BY GINA PELLEGRINI

TAKE INITIATIVE & SUCCEED!

Pellegrini Team Consulting
8945 Aztec Drive
Eden Prairie, MN 55347
(952) 829-5300 | www.pellegriniteam.com

TABLE OF CONTENTS

"Doing your best means never stop trying."

Author Unknown

INTRODUCTION

Before I started my own company, I worked for 17 years as an assistant to a successful financial advisor in Chicago. So much of who I am as a business owner and consultant can be traced to those early years of my career. I know what it's like to work for a boss with a strong work ethic but little interest (initially) in communication and teamwork. I know how to make calls, cultivate clients and schedule appointments like a pro. Just as important, I know how to create an environment where the staff is empowered and the boss is supported.

When I began the job, I was unsure of myself. I received minimal training and really didn't have a clue about my actual role. Basically, I learned my duties by trial and error because there wasn't anyone in our office in the same position. I gradually gained confidence and the experience to take over new and more challenging responsibilities. How did this happen? To a certain extent, I just took the plunge, but I can also point to a pivotal event that changed my attitude and motivation.

One day a client called with a very specific question. I didn't know the answer, and my boss was not very helpful. He wanted me to be more proactive and self-sufficient. I started to dig around to find the answer and discovered there were more resources available than I thought. I not only found the answer to the client's question, I also stumbled across my role. My purpose was to get the answers and make things happen behind the scenes in the business.

To run the office efficiently, I suggested everything go through me, from incoming calls, mail, voice mail, email, etc. I listened to my employer whenever he was on the phone and got a feel for what he needed, when and why. In fact, there were times when he requested certain things for a client meeting and I did the opposite because I knew what he said was not what he meant. We developed a unique, successful form of communication.

Why did I stay for 17 years? Because I was trusted, involved, challenged, rewarded and relied upon by my employer. Did I make mistakes? Absolutely. Did I learn from them? Always. Did my boss second guess what I was doing or how I was doing it? Sometimes -- he's only human! But once I learned to run the office and take the initiative, we became an unbeatable team.

Although it's in their best interest, employers don't always establish a culture of trust and independence. Letting go and trusting staff is very difficult for most employers. But you can shape your career destiny by believing in yourself and influencing events. Look around your office with fresh eyes. How can you help move the company forward? How can you support your boss? What can you do differently? What duties can you take over to allow your employer to be more productive? Challenge yourself to take on more responsibilities. Your job is to make life easier for your boss, and by doing so, everyone wins.

The way I see it, if your situation is imperfect -- maybe your boss is uncommunicative, volatile or a control freak -- you have three options. (1) You can accept the status quo and continue to complain under your breath. (2) You can quit. (3) You can improve the situation by looking for solutions and understanding your purpose at work.

Which option works for you?

I hope this book encourages you to look for solutions and understand your purpose. It's your future, so take the initiative and succeed!

1. UNDERSTANDING Your Boss

"I've always found that the speed of the boss is the speed of the team."

Lee Iacocca

Before I discuss your purpose, let's look at your workplace. What "type" of manager is your boss?

When I conduct teamwork workshops around the country, I often talk about the various managerial types. Why? Because most employers don't understand how they come across as managers or why their staff is truly looking for guidance and leadership.

During this part of the workshop, I display a list of the most common managerial types and read it aloud. People in the audience begin to squirm in their seats. The business owners smile sheepishly (or grimace) and the employees nod their heads in agreement. I then ask the employees to select the descriptions that apply to their boss.

Now I'm asking you -- which managerial type(s) is your boss? Circle all that apply!

The Micromanagers

...need to be involved in everything. They're convinced no one can do anything as well as they can. They tend to hover, interrupt and always question what you're working on.

The Changeable Managers

...switch direction constantly and often abruptly. Most of the time, you can't follow their thought process, and because they're so random, you don't know if you should follow their lead or just wait awhile because something's bound to change.

The Delegating Managers

...delegate everything, big or small, because they trust your capabilities and know you'll follow through.

The Hyper Managers

...are constantly on the move and tend to do things at the last minute. They lose focus easily and are so busy, they rarely have time for you.

The Unpredictable Managers

...are impulsive and inconsistent. They rarely stick to the plan and often delegate with limited information or unrealistic time frames. As a result, you're never sure what the day will bring.

The Mixed-Message Managers

...say one thing and do another. They can be evasive, indecisive and erratic.

The Unreadable Managers

...are hard to decipher. They keep things to themselves and expect you to read their minds. You sense their frustration, but it's impossible to know if their dissatisfaction relates to you.

The Hands-Off Managers

...are uninvolved, easily distracted and lack direction or vision.

The Involved Managers

...include you in the vision of the company, delegate consistently and let you do your job. They encourage growth, communicate openly, listen to what you have to say and treat you like their #1 client.

How many types did you circle? The average assistant circles four. The main reason I included the managerial types is to help you understand how most business owners are a combination of types. Their behavior is the product of their temperament, work habits and outlook. Business owners have strengths in many areas but for the most part, managing people is *not* one of them.

Is it wrong to be a certain type of manager? Not at all. The key, however, is to make sure employees understand how, or more importantly why employers operate as they do. You can help your boss break through self-imposed barriers if you understand the underlying type(s). With your help, your boss can become The Involved Manager, which is the ideal! The goal is to convince your boss to delegate everything possible, trust you to get the work done and involve you in the company vision. When this happens, you'll build a cohesive team in which combined effort is valued.

Don't worry. Throughout the book, I'll continue to include effective strategies for handling the various managerial types.

OVERVIEW

✗ Figure out what you're dealing with. If you understand the managerial "types," you're better prepared to help your boss become an Involved or Delegating Manager. This may take some time, but it's worth the effort. In the meantime, don't take your employer's actions personally.

2. Your PURPOSE at Work

Purpose

> **1.** the reason for which anything is done, created or exists
> **2.** a fixed design, outcome or idea that is the object of an action or other effort

World English Dictionary

Do you know why you were hired? Do you understand your true purpose at work?

When people think about their jobs, they tend to focus on specific activities. Very few employees understand the big picture. They think, "I'm an administrative assistant," or whatever their title is, and zero in on concrete job responsibilities. They unconsciously put limitations on their role. I'm asking you to step back and think beyond specific tasks. What is the real reason you're on the team?

From my perspective, your purpose is to simplify your employer's daily routine. When employers delegate responsibilities to their staff, they gain the freedom to focus on the business. You were hired to free up your boss's time, and because of you, your boss can concentrate on bringing in new clients, prospecting and being in front of people.

Your purpose, however, goes beyond the daily tasks. As you learn more about the business, you can take on a more proactive role. Remember, when employers spend time on the wrong things or are disorganized, the business suffers. And when the business suffers, so does the bottom line. It's up to you to think ahead, take over as much as possible and eliminate any bottlenecks preventing business growth. A more active role is especially important if letting go is an issue for your boss! Yes, this may sound like a tall order, but if you want a long-term career with a lot of upside potential, this is your best course of action.

What is the upside potential? It's the promise of greater involvement and financial reward when you contribute more directly to the company's profits. When you're truly making a difference, and the business grows because of your efforts, you have a real stake in the company's success. Another plus -- you actually *enjoy* going to work every day.

I learned this early in my career as an administrative assistant. When I first started, I was paid a base salary. After a couple of years, my pay formula changed; I began getting a bonus incentive for specific results. I decided to take a risk by exchanging salary increases for a (possibly) bigger payoff with bonus incentives. It was a smart gamble as I earned more each year based on our business growth. I was excited about those extra dollars in my paycheck. My financial risk motivated me to constantly manage my boss's time so he could focus on bringing in the money. Again, when employers are freed up, everyone wins!

As an assistant, I learned there's a big difference between doing my job and achieving my purpose. If I gained more knowledge, earned appropriate licenses and filtered everything that came into the office so my boss didn't get bogged down, I made things easier for him and played a substantial part in the business growth.

I challenge you to think about your own work habits. Do you make life less complicated for your boss -- or do you forget your purpose? Do you take the initiative whenever possible -- or do you wait for help or instructions? Are you willing to try new things -- or do you stick to the same old game plan? Are you upbeat and committed to your work -- or do you drag people down with your negative attitude? Do you consider what's best for the business -- or just what's best for you?

People don't always understand the impact of their actions. Let's look at some specific work habits and activities. Are you one of those employees who shows up late for work? Transfers calls to your boss's voice mail without asking questions? Allows important things to fall through the cracks because you focus on less important tasks that don't bring in money or move the business? Do you make mistakes because you're not taking time to review your work?

Think about the implications of your actions. Basically, if you're doing some or all of these things, you're not supporting your boss. If you're chronically late, your boss probably interprets your behavior as disrespect or disregard for the business. This can affect your interaction and the role you play on the team. When you automatically put calls into voice mail, your boss is inconvenienced; he or she has to take time to listen to the messages when more than likely, you can handle most of them. When things fall through the cracks, the business loses momentum. When prioritizing tasks, you want to focus on the most important activities in the morning -- scheduling appointments, submitting paperwork for new business and preparing for appointments -- and in the afternoon, on client service, correspondence, database management, etc. Finally, if you're careless about mistakes, your boss will begin to check your work, and that's *not* a good use of your boss's time.

What if you were an employer? How would you handle these situations? Wouldn't you think they were an irritating waste of time and money?

Try to see the big picture. Instead of "me," think of "we." Get involved in the business, bring value, make it about teamwork. Ultimately, employees get more of what they need at work if they give their bosses more of what they want. Make their day!

At Pellegrini Team Consulting, each member of my team understands their purpose and how it contributes to the reputation, direction and success of the business.

Lynne, a longtime team member, explains her purpose this way: "As a business writer, my job is to work with Gina to help her formulate and express her many ideas. Over the years, we've come up with a process that allows Gina to get her thoughts on paper. Together, we hash over ideas, rework main points, fine-tune drafts and eventually arrive at a finished product. Throughout the writing process, communication is nonstop. The way I see it, my job is to deliver information that explains, enhances and promotes the business. If I fulfill my professional purpose, Gina has more time to spend on things that matter most -- her consulting, phone seminars and speaking engagements. I appreciate the trust and respect she has for everyone on the team, and of course, I get a kick out of her enthusiasm."

Laurel, our Consulting and Hiring Coordinator, is my go-to person for business planning, scheduling and client relations. She helps me stay on top of everything! Laurel says, "My purpose is to help Gina run the business as efficiently as possible. To me, everything I do reflects upon Gina and our company. I try to anticipate problems and step in whenever Gina's workload gets too heavy. For example, soon after I started here, I took over our hiring services because it drained too much of Gina's time. Now I handle hiring while Gina concentrates on other revenue-generating activities. We're always working together toward a common goal."

Remember, what's good for the business is ultimately good for you.

OVERVIEW

✘ Understand the difference between doing your job and fulfilling your purpose at work.

✘ Remember why you were hired. Your primary purpose is to simplify your employer's daily schedule. In other words, you were hired to free up your boss's time.

✘ Think ahead. If you're one step ahead of your boss, the office will run more smoothly and productivity will increase. What's good for the business is ultimately good for you!

3. The Role of COMMUNICATION

"Communication -- the human connection -- is the key to personal and career success."

Paul J. Meyer

Good communication at work is a precondition for taking the initiative. Without regular discussions between you and your boss, you won't know what's expected or why. How can you go beyond your job description if you haven't discussed the duties and/or expectations? How can you think like your boss if you never talk about the finer points of the business? (Or even the basics!) How can you feel involved and valued if no one gives you feedback on your performance? How can you help the company grow if you're not aware of the company vision?

Communication is vital to success, but for many people, it's a real challenge! When everyone is busy, it's easy to overlook or avoid true communication. People don't take the time to talk about the right things at the right time. Some fear speaking their minds because they're uncomfortable with confrontation. Others are concerned about hurt feelings and misunderstandings. Still others are unsure about how to address an issue.

Unintentionally, some types of managers are poor at communication.

Unreadable Managers are difficult because they're guarded and unsure how to express their thoughts. Hyper Managers are tricky to work with because they don't take time to focus their thoughts or examine the issues.

The Unreadable Manager presents special challenges. Do you ever feel something is wrong at work, or your boss is frustrated -- but you're not sure why? Do you wonder if it has something to do with you? If so, you've probably got a classic Unreadable Manager on your hands. Your best bet is to ask questions. "Is everything okay? You seem upset. Is there anything I can do to help? Have I done something that's frustrating you?" Simple questions can open up a dialogue between you and your employer. Each baby step leads to better communication in the future.

When it comes to helping employers change habits, I've walked the walk. After I'd worked with my advisor for a couple of months, we began scheduling a weekly meeting. It took awhile to get the hang of it! Every Monday morning I'd walk in prepared, but when I sat down, my employer would pick up the phone or begin working on something else. Because I wasn't sure what to do, I sat and waited for his attention, which sometimes took 20 minutes. I was frustrated during these so-called meetings because I had work to do. So whenever I felt tuned out, I'd ask pointedly, "Should I come back when you're ready?" Eventually, he got it and focused on the meeting. I learned to walk in and start the meeting, regardless of what he was doing. Within a couple of minutes, he got involved.

If you feel communication is not working for you, find ways to change the environment. Maybe your employer has a problem telling it like it is which leaves you wondering what's going on. You can feel the tension in the office but you can't do anything about it because you're not sure if it's you, a client or something going on in your boss's personal life. Or maybe your employer speaks without a filter or takes jabs at you when things aren't working. Maybe your boss fails to praise you for a job well done. All signs of a poor communicator!

Help your boss become a better communicator by scheduling weekly meetings. The meetings should last about one-half hour and include an agenda. Some agenda ideas: focus for the week, accountability, workflow and update of the company goals. Be prepared and don't bring up unimportant information or obstacles. You don't want to give your boss an excuse to skip the meeting. The weekly sessions are about movement and forward thinking which will keep your boss involved and attentive.

I also recommend two 15-minute updates each day. The 15-minute meetings -- one in the morning and the other in the afternoon -- help eliminate interruptions and increase productivity. They also give you an opportunity to ask questions or prioritize workflow.

The point is to communicate consistently so you're on the same page. Of course, to really communicate, you need to listen to each other! Someone once said, "We have two ears and one mouth so that we can listen twice as much as we speak." I tell assistants to *hear* what their boss is saying and to insist politely that their boss do the same.

With effective communication, you can...

✖ Recognize your purpose in the business

✖ Understand your boss's management style

✖ Develop trust

✖ Take ownership of your role

✖ Take the initiative

Without it, you'll be frustrated at work.

OVERVIEW

✗ Understand the "type" of manager you're working with. You'll be better equipped to handle your boss's habits -- both the good ones and the bad ones -- and you'll get a lot more done.

✗ Use daily and weekly meetings to promote better communication. Keep the sessions brief and focused on forward progress.

✗ Be present at the meetings. That means everyone! Listen carefully to what is said -- and respond. According to Roger Sessions, "Communication is two-sided -- vital and profound communication makes demands on those who are to receive it..." *Both* employers and employees should be ready to meet the demands of communication. It's give and take.

4. A Matter of TRUST

"The glue that holds all relationships together -- including the relationship between the leader and the led -- is trust..."

Brian Tracy

Is trust an issue in your office? So many people I work with -- employers *and* employees alike -- are concerned about the lack of trust in their office.

Why is letting go and developing trust so tough? Over the years, I've learned many employers worry they'll get burned if they trust their employees. The way they see it, an employee in charge could resign, do a lazy job or disrupt the business -- and then where would they be? Also, for many employers, there's a fear of losing control. How will they know if workflow is prioritized correctly or if things are getting done the "right" way? How will they know if clients are cared for?

Most employers lack trust because the business is their livelihood and future. If there's a mistake or something falls through the cracks, it's on their shoulders. They've assumed the risk and take it very seriously as you would if it were your business.

Yet when I speak with my clients across the country, it always baffles me that trust, or lack of it, is such a hurdle. Why would you hire someone to assist you in your business and not trust them? Even worse, why would you undermine your own employees with your distrust? If someone in the office makes a mistake that results in constant suspicion and surveillance, how will that employee ever take the initiative?

After reading about the different managerial types in Chapter One, you can probably predict which types struggle the most in this area. (Is lack of trust at the root of the Unreadable Manager's behavior?)

If employees aren't trusted, they'll *never* feel empowered to go beyond what's expected of them. In my workshops, I tell business owners that no matter why they have trust issues, the result is the same: "*Your staff mirrors you!*" Not in terms of work ethic, attitude or knowledge, but trust. This usually makes them pause and think. I tell them that when employees feel trusted -- and employers give them the time and attention they need -- they will in turn trust their boss and feel empowered to take the initiative. Otherwise, it's going to be tough to build a thriving business.

When I was an assistant, I was fortunate to have a boss who trusted me right away, or so I thought! Actually, he didn't think or worry about what I was doing because he was so focused on building the business. He just hoped for the best. However, sometimes my employer's lack of involvement made me feel mistrusted. I soon learned it wasn't a trust issue; he simply didn't know what to do with me or how to manage me. At any rate, we seemed to earn each other's trust. My boss delegated everything to me, and because he did, I tried my best to meet and even exceed his expectations.

Does your boss trust you? If you can honestly say yes, appreciate your situation because unfortunately, it's not necessarily the norm. If you feel your boss struggles with trust issues, you're not alone and it may not be your fault.

How can you break through the trust barrier?

First you need to figure out why there's an issue. Have you made a lot of mistakes? Do you spend time on the Internet for personal use during the work day? Are you coming in late or leaving early when your boss is out of the office? Do you talk with friends when you should be working? Do you do what you say you're going to do? Have things fallen through the cracks?

These are *some* of the reasons employers lack trust. So again, put yourself in your boss's shoes. Are you doing something that erodes trust?

Find out! Talk to your boss. Have an honest discussion about how this lack of trust makes you feel. I know it's not easy, but what do you have to lose? My motto is *go for the gold* because if you're unhappy, you probably won't stay. You may be surprised at your boss's response because in most cases, employers aren't sure if or why they have a trust issue.

If it is something you've done, find ways to regain your boss's trust by demonstrating your skill set, reliability and confidence. Explain, explore and expand what you do. Share your progress and results with your boss, and eventually, trust will develop or no longer be an issue.

Of course, lack of trust goes both ways, and employees don't always trust their employers. Can you relate? Are you carrying around a past experience or resenting your current boss for a particular reason? One of the surest ways to ruin an employee's trust is for a boss to break a promise. As a consultant, I've seen the fallout when this happens. A client of mine had employed a great marketing assistant for several years. One day he promised her an amazing gift if they hit a huge goal. Unfortunately, when they hit the goal, he backed out of the deal. Talk about breaking someone's trust. They were never the same again.

If it's hard for you to trust your boss because of a past experience, let go of the memory and give your current boss the benefit of the doubt. Or share your concerns to help develop more trust.

I really like this quote about trust from Bert Dedecker: "The most important language in effective communicating is an almost unspoken language, the language of trust." Trust is worth earning and keeping.

Find ways to understand each other's trust issues. Examine the unknown fears and build trust through honest and consistent communication.

OVERVIEW

✗ Understand that an employer's fear of letting go and trusting employees is detrimental to the business. Roger Staubach, a successful real estate entrepreneur after his pro football career, pointed out, "If you don't have trust inside your company, then you can't transfer it to your customers."

✗ Get to the root of the problem. Be honest about trust issues in your office and their origins. Then work together to build faith and confidence in each other.

5. #1 PRIORITY

Priority

1. a thing that is regarded as more important than another
2. the fact or condition of being regarded or treated as more important
3. the right to take precedence or to proceed before others

Google English Dictionary

Who's your #1 client? By that, I mean who's the person with the biggest impact on the business?

It should be your boss! In fact, I like to tell business owners and employees that they should be each others's #1 client. Given your purpose in the business, that's how you should look at it. Your boss comes first. SPFs -- **s**upporting, **p**rotecting, **f**iltering and **s**cheduling everything for your boss -- is your primary goal. (More on SPFs later!)

I know what you're thinking. I'm here to take care of the clients. That's true -- but don't drop everything to handle a client issue, unless it's urgent. When you do, you push aside important work for your boss. If that work isn't done, your boss becomes frustrated, things get backlogged, and you feel overwhelmed.

Let me give you an example. One of the things we do at Pellegrini

Team Consulting is teach marketing assistants how to schedule appointments to fill up their employers' calendars. We recommend spending an hour a day -- 9:00 to 10:00 a.m. -- to make daily calls for appointments. However, about 85% of the time, assistants tell me they don't have time to phone because there's too much stuff to do. They say the interruptions and workload don't allow them to make the dials.

They're not understanding their purpose. If their job is to make calls and fill the calendar with a steady stream of appointments, then that's what they should be doing! Putting off calls because of client service or administrative work defeats their purpose. Being in front of clients to bring in revenue is the top priority of their boss -- their #1 client.

Yes, as an assistant, you have a lot on your plate, and sometimes you're overwhelmed. But better you than your employer. Your boss has invested a lot in you to encourage continued business growth. It's your job to find a way to put your boss and income activities first.

For successful teams, the most important job is to keep your boss on task. How? With **SPFs** -- **S**upporting their needs, **P**rotecting their time, **F**iltering anything that comes through the office, and most important, **S**cheduling/managing all of their time.

What does this involve?

Support

Everything at the office should be geared toward your boss's needs. In other words, you're supporting your boss in every situation. It's your job to keep stuff off his/her desk and to figure out what's needed next. It's up to you to make sure your boss is ready for appointments. It's your responsibility to follow up after client meetings; don't wait for your boss to delegate tasks. By taking the initiative -- thinking ahead, planning well and moving things along -- you provide true support for your employer. A lot more is accomplished, and the business continues to grow.

Protect

Your boss's time is crucial for business growth. In my view, your boss should concentrate on two things -- talking/meeting with clients and prospecting. Everything else can be delegated to staff. Protect your boss's time by meeting twice a day to review work and handle questions. By doing so, you reduce interruptions and maximize your boss's time. With scheduled meetings, you are more prepared to go over things. It's important to keep your boss in the loop, especially about key tasks that have been delegated. I suggest holding off with bad news until the end of the day so your boss is totally present during appointments. If you're protective, everyone is more productive.

F ilter

This one is extremely important. If you filter phone calls, mail, emails and voice mail, you'll save your boss all kinds of time. Communication should be handled promptly but not by your boss. When something is truly important, and your employer's involvement is necessary, you can set up a time during the day (your 15 minute meeting) to discuss the issue. Otherwise, handle all incoming requests and questions by yourself. By filtering office communications, you'll earn the trust of the clients, and things will get done quicker because you're eliminating your boss as the middleman. As you pick up the phone or read an email, think of yourself as a private investigator. By doing so, you'll learn to handle all kinds of things without the involvement of your employer.

Schedule

Again, how you schedule your employer's time has a real impact on the business. One way to manage time efficiently is by filling time slots on the calendar for things only your boss can do. For example, two or three days before a scheduled appointment, reserve a time slot for your boss to review the files you've prepared. This way, any changes can be done systematically, rather than in a mad scramble at the last minute. If it's your responsibility to schedule client meetings, find out how many appointments are needed and what kind. Then fill the calendar accordingly. While filtering calls, if you think someone should speak to your boss, schedule a time to do so. If you fill the time slots wisely, your boss can work on the right things at the right time.

Again, your boss is your #1 client because everything hinges on his or her success. If at times your boss is frustrating or unappreciative, remember the synchronicity. When your boss does well, the company does well, and so do you.

OVERVIEW

X Put your boss first. Obviously, clients are important, but if your boss is swamped and things aren't getting done, your clients won't get the attention they deserve. Focus first on your boss and the income tasks -- then handle everything else.

X Understand the investment. You were hired to free up your employer's time.

X Practice **SPFs**. Make it a point to **S**upport, **P**rotect, **F**ilter and **S**chedule your boss.

6. OWNERSHIP of Your Job

Ownership

    1. the state or fact of being an owner
    2. legal right of possession; proprietorship

World English Dictionary

What does it mean to "take ownership"? It means approaching your job with the same sense of pride, satisfaction and responsibility that you'd feel as a property owner. It means trying your hardest because your job is a reflection of you. F. John Reh said it best: "Any job you do is going to 'have your fingerprints all over it.' That is why it is so important to take ownership of your job, any job you do, and really own it. Do it the best you can; do it the best it can be done. That is how you succeed."

I work with business owners every day, and the one thing I hear all the time is how much they want their staff to take ownership and the initiative. Ownership and initiative sound similar, but in my mind, they're different.

"Taking ownership" means treating your job with the same interest and sense of responsibility you'd have when buying a house. You'd fix breakdowns, solve internal issues and keep things clean and orderly.

Ownership at work is similar because as you care for things, you get the benefit of a well-tended, well-run office. If you manage your boss's time, keep things on track and monitor workflow closely, you make things easier for your boss and definitely make a difference. Find ways to make that happen. Remember, as you manage the office, your employer can manage the growth of the company. That's ownership on both sides!

Of course, this is easier said than done. For a variety of reasons, it's hard for some of you to take ownership. Do any of these sound familiar?

X I just want to do my job -- no more, no less.

X I don't know enough about the business.

X I don't want to make a mistake.

Let's break down these barriers to ownership.

I just want to do my job -- no more, no less.

When I was 21, that was my attitude. Most days I'd show up on time, do my work and leave promptly at 5 o'clock. Technically, that's what I was paid to do, but with that attitude, I would never get ahead. I soon realized that with a little extra effort and ownership, I'd become more valuable to my boss and the company. I discovered the difference between a job and a career which is why I stayed there for 17 years.

I'm not saying you have to work longer hours to do the job. I'm saying you have to maximize your impact during the time you're there. Stretch your thinking!

Your boss takes on the risk and responsibility of running a business. You can take on more responsibility without the downside (risk) and grow as a valued asset to the business. Wouldn't you rather have a career than a job? Most business owners want their employees to learn more and become more involved. It opens new doors for all parties involved. If you don't expand your role, the business might decline or your boss might outgrow you and find someone else who wants more responsibility and growth.

When I first started as an administrative assistant, I was thrown into appointment scheduling on my very first day. I wasn't sure I was going to like it, but I didn't have much choice. After three months, I found it fun, challenging and rewarding. Over time I took that responsibility away from my boss, and it was my pathway to a challenging career, an increase in income and true recognition in the business. Who knows, by taking more ownership, you could discover things you never thought you'd enjoy. "Learning never exhausts the mind," according to Leonardo da Vinci.

I don't know enough about the business.

Valid point, but if you don't find ways to get more involved, you're never going to learn. Face the fact that most employers don't take time to train their staff. Job knowledge and skills are often self-taught. So make it your goal to learn something new every month, regardless of how long you've been in the business. Are there books you can read, technology you can learn, licenses to obtain? Can you attend company training sessions or take online courses? There are plenty of resources out there. Just do the research and figure out what's best for you and make an impact on the business.

When I supported my employer, the best training was listening to him talk to clients on the phone and watching him complete proposals and paperwork. I learned a lot and eventually felt comfortable doing more. Knowledge gives you confidence, and when you're confident, the sky's the limit.

I don't want to make a mistake.

Nobody does -- but mistakes happen. Often, mistakes occur because you feel rushed and out of time. If you prioritize your work, however, you'll have time to do things thoroughly *and* review your work. When you type a letter or prepare for an appointment, it's imperative to double check your work. It's your job, so it's up to *you* to be accurate. This gets back to ownership. Arrange your day so work is done systematically, and you aren't rushing around at the last minute. Remember, if mistakes are made, your boss will be embarrassed or think it's necessary to always check your work. That's a waste of everyone's time.

If you make a mistake, my advice is to own up to it, learn from it and never let it disable you. Mistakes can be instructional. When you make an error -- and then fix it -- you're on the alert for next time. You probably won't make the mistake again because you'll know what to look for and avoid.

Taking ownership increases your involvement and job satisfaction and improves overall productivity. When you excel at your role and make things easier for your boss, you become invaluable. So stretch yourself and don't be afraid to try new things. As Jim Goodwin says, "Take ownership of the job; the impossible is often the untried."

OVERVIEW

✗ Stretch yourself. Embrace your responsibilities and don't just get by.

✗ Always look for ways to expand your involvement and ownership.

✗ Don't worry about occasional mistakes. No one's perfect, and we all learn from our missteps. Remember what Jack Welch said: "Mistakes can often be as good a teacher as success."

7. INITIATIVE to Succeed!

Initiative

> **1.** the power or ability to begin or to follow through energetically with a plan or task; enterprise and determination
>
> **2.** a beginning or introductory step; an opening move: *took the initiative in trying to solve the problem*

TheFreeDictionary

Why is initiative so important and what does it really mean?

Most employees don't understand why they should grab the reins and expand their role. Too often they place limitations on themselves and stay stuck in the status quo. Or they *think* they're taking the initiative when in reality, they're following the same old habits and routine.

"Taking the initiative" is thinking outside the box, looking for better ways to do things and creating solutions when obstacles arise. It means taking tasks *away* from your employer to save them time. Go beyond what's delegated; handle their voice mail, schedule their time, run interference and keep them on track.

You might be thinking, "My plate is full! I can't do more." Not really. The point is to reduce your boss's involvement in tasks that don't generate income.

I know it's not easy to take the initiative, but if you give it a shot, you can turn your job into a satisfying, long-term career. That is, if you want to! Even if you're a longtime employee, there are still plenty of ways to take the initiative. The question is, how?

Employers say they want proactive involvement, but that's easier said than done. It's not like you get much instruction or feedback from them. Business owners go into business for various reasons, but as we know, managing people is neither their strength nor interest. They do realize, however, that they can't grow the business alone which is why they hire professionals like you.

As mentioned in the Introduction, I began to take the initiative when a client called our office with a question I couldn't answer. Remember, my purpose at work was to free up my employer's time. Instead of asking my boss, I made a couple of calls on my own, and voila, I found the answer. Throughout the years, I continued to take on more and looked for ways to free up his time.

When my employee Annie started working at Pellegrini Team Consulting, she really hit the ground running. During her first day on the job, I discussed employment guidelines, her job description and my own expectations. I casually mentioned my interest in increasing the company's involvement in social media. Details were vague. At her one-month review, Annie showed me what she had done with social media, and I was impressed. She'd set up Facebook, LinkedIn and Twitter without any direction or input from me. It was great! Even though no one trained her or provided guidance, she jumped in. Now that's initiative!

You may be thinking, "This doesn't apply to me. I already take the initiative." But do you really? If so, how? Remember, when I'm referring to initiative, it means going beyond your everyday responsibilities.

Before I delve any deeper, let's examine how *employers* think and operate in ways that stifle initiative. Too many bosses:

- are afraid to let go
- are micromanagers
- constantly change their minds
- don't listen to suggestions
- delegate at the last minute
- don't provide any kind of training

Let's look at these situations.

My employer is afraid to let go.

Do you understand how difficult it is for most employers to let go and trust their employees? For the most part, this has nothing to do with you. It's just their nature. It's simply ingrained in some people to do things themselves even though they have a qualified employee who can handle the tasks. You'd think this would be a non-issue since the point of hiring someone like you is to delegate as much as possible to free up their time for income-producing activities. But many employers are control freaks who do a lot of the work because they have trust issues.

How can you get past this barrier? Try discussing the situation with your boss to uncover their fears. I'm not saying this will be an easy conversation. Some employers don't understand they're doing tasks you could handle. If they don't let go, you'll never be able to go beyond what's expected of you. Refer to Chapter Nine for scripts to help you with this conversation.

My employer is a micromanager.

Yes, most of them are! Again, it has nothing to do with you. Micromanagers become unnecessarily involved in everything. They usually "help" you because they're unsure of your skill set, knowledge or follow through. Or they're concerned you'll do something differently than they would. Regardless of their reasons, help them get out of your way by proving yourself and showing that your self-sufficiency makes financial sense. In Chapter Nine, I have scripts you can use if you work with a micromanager.

Maybe you're thinking, "My boss is a micromanager. Why fight it?" Because if you don't, you'll complain, feel frustrated or even leave your job because you're not using your skills. Remember, we're talking about initiative here, so if *you* don't believe change is possible, your boss will never budge. Your involvement and attitude make a huge difference. I know your boss can change, but not without some help from you.

Show some initiative by letting your boss know about the micromanaging. Let's say you walk into your boss's office with a question about work delegated to you. Instead of answering your question, your boss says, "Give me the file, I'll take care of it." You're not asking your boss to do the work! Sometimes an employer thinks questions are your way of saying, "I don't know how to do this." Then they take back the task. So speak up if your boss tries to reclaim an assignment you're perfectly capable of handling. Remind them of your purpose. You're there to do the work so they stay in front of people.

Continue to take the initiative by becoming a filter for everything that comes into the office -- mail, calls, people, etc. When you reduce interruptions and demonstrate your competence, your boss will stop micromanaging and become a better leader.

My employer constantly changes his/her mind.

In most offices, the staff prefers routine and consistency. If the systems and day-to-day routine are working, why change them? However, most business owners thrive on change, and I'm one of them. (We're talking about The Hyper or Changeable Manager!) I'm always thinking of different ways to grow the business, create new products and make things better for our clients. My team is used to me changing my mind or shifting gears, but in the beginning, I'm sure they rolled their eyes and wondered why. Today they understand this is who I am and how I expand the business *with* their involvement. True, no one likes to spend hours on a project just to have it shelved or dismantled because their boss changes course. (Guilty!) But business owners aren't trying to frustrate you. It's just the way they operate. Their energy and ideas propelled them to become business owners. So do your best to roll with them by being flexible and doing whatever you can to help them implement their ideas.

My employer doesn't listen to suggestions.

Are you sure? Or is that simply what you think? When I first started as an assistant, I had all sorts of ideas to improve our workflow. In the beginning, my ideas weren't taken seriously, but I didn't give up. Over time, I took the initiative and found ways to implement my ideas without my boss's input. Once he saw how my suggestions made a difference, he began to listen to me. Eventually, he understood that I was the one doing the actual work, so if I found a "better way," it became the new way. My initiative paid off.

Fortunately, I was never criticized for my suggestions or efforts, but I know plenty of assistants who are. They take the initiative and then get grilled about it. Once they're questioned, they feel defeated. They become hesitant and do only what they're told to do. If that's the case, talk to your boss. Explain why it's important for you to find ways to make things more efficient since your job is to run the office. As Eric Harvey said, "People tend to work harder for their own ideas. Solutions they participate in developing become commitments that are much more likely to yield quick and permanent results."

An employer who doesn't listen to the staff's ideas is often The Mixed-Message Manager. If your boss tells you to take the initiative, then reacts negatively when you do, you're put on the defensive. All I can say is give it some time. Your employer may need to get comfortable with your self-reliance, and eventually, he or she will be glad you're not waiting for directions. In the meantime, continue to think outside the box. Eventually, your boss will recognize your contributions and truly listen to your ideas.

My employer delegates at the last minute.

Frustrating, isn't it? This is where taking the initiative can make a real difference. Delegating at the last minute is more common than you think, and it happens a lot with the Changeable Manager and the Hyper Manager. Many employers are convinced they think better when delegating at the last minute. However, this is how mistakes happen or important workflow gets pushed aside. To address the problem, try to uncover why your boss procrastinates and how you can help him/her prepare in advance. Then point out the advantages of planning ahead.

One way to take the initiative is to say, "I checked the calendar. You have an appointment with John on Thursday. What do you need for the meeting?" If you anticipate the work and talk to your boss in advance, things will move more smoothly. Eventually, your direct involvement in the appointment prep and other tasks will become the norm.

One last thing, don't be afraid to share your concerns about the likelihood of mistakes if you have to rush through work delegated at the last minute.

My employer didn't provide any kind of training.

I know this is a huge problem -- I have firsthand experience! When I was an assistant, my employer really didn't train me on anything. Although I assumed he would offer some general guidance, I realized after a few weeks that I was on my own. Making calls for appointments, completing paperwork, handling client service, etc. -- I had to figure out everything by myself. Many people would throw their hands in the air and get frustrated but instead, I felt challenged to learn the ropes myself.

Let me share an example. When I began calling for appointments, I phoned existing clients only. One day I asked my boss why I wasn't calling the referrals. He said he wanted to call them himself because they were his bread and butter. If I were making those calls and lost potential clients, the business wouldn't grow. It was clear he wasn't going to let go of the referrals, train me or concede that I might get better results than he did.

But over time, the referrals began to collect dust because my boss didn't get to them. Both he and I were on the phone, making appointments to fill his calendar. As the referrals piled up, I began to think differently. I knew I could help if I went beyond what was expected of me. So one day I took the initiative and began calling the referrals, without any training. Yes, I was a bit over my head at first, but in time I taught myself how to overcome the objections and get the appointments.

How did my boss react? At first he was very concerned about my results. But when he realized that referrals were just sitting on his desk, going nowhere, he agreed that calls from me were better than no calls at all. How would I have handled the situation if he'd been upset? I would have discussed my reasoning, shared my results and/or asked for more time to prove myself. But it did work, and the end result was that he never picked up the phone again!

Two things happened here. I saw a need -- and I took the initiative. I realized I could make a difference in the business by going beyond the parameters of my job. By stepping outside the box, I found I truly enjoyed the challenge of the referral calls. In fact I enjoyed it so much that today I train people to be as confident as I was in making those calls. Ideally, a boss should provide solid training, but if that doesn't happen, you can still succeed.

If your boss thinks and operates in any of these ways, what can you do to help? Start by working on the way *you* think and operate! The question to ask yourself -- the one that applies in all cases -- is "What else can I do?" What tasks can you take over to free up your employer's time? How can you become more valuable to the business? How can you be the go-to resource for clients?

Let me give you some basic examples of taking the initiative:

✗When the phone rings, you have a perfect opportunity to jump in. In most cases, the caller will ask for your boss or their voice mail. Unless it's a return call, instead of transferring it, handle the call yourself. Approach it as if your employer is not available, even if he or she is. Simply say, "_____ is unavailable right now. How may I help you?" If you can handle the issue, do so. If you don't know the answer to a question, be resourceful. If the caller really needs to talk to your boss, don't take a message but schedule a time for them to speak. By jumping in, you build credibility with clients, learn something new and most important, reduce interruptions for your boss who can then stay focused on growing the business.

✗When clients call in for service, go one step beyond their needs. Let's say someone calls in to change a beneficiary. The average assistant would simply send the proper form to the client. But by taking the initiative, you might end up with helpful information that leads to more business. What's a better way to handle the situation? Try this: "I'd be more than happy to take care of this for you. Let's fill out the form over the phone. Then I'll send it to you for your signature." By completing the form together, you'll find out on the spot about an important change such as marriage, death, new baby, etc. It could be a perfect time to schedule an appointment. End your conversation with the client by saying, "Based on this change, I feel it would be beneficial for you to come in for a review. While you're here, you can sign the form. What day works best for you?"

✗ Be on top of your job and precise when communicating with your employer. When your boss asks a question, be prepared to answer it! A client of mine was frustrated with his assistant when she said, "Tom wants to talk with you as soon as possible." (Tom is their best client.) My client's first question: "What does Tom want?" Unfortunately, the assistant couldn't remember and didn't write it down. Her boss was irritated because he felt his assistant should be prepared for such a basic, legitimate question. I agree. Stay on top of your tasks and be ready to give your boss accurate and complete information. When you're asked about a specific project or client, it's good to know your stuff. When you act like you have no idea, your boss panics. Know what you're working on and where you're at with it. Remember, your purpose is to make things easier for your boss. You're in charge of running the office, keeping things moving and making sure nothing falls through the cracks.

✘ Instead of bombarding your boss with questions all day, review things together twice a day. Workflow is smoother if you meet in your boss's office to go over things. Important: be sure to walk out the door with everything you walked in with. Get out of the habit of putting things in your boss's In Box or on their desk. Leave nothing behind! These regular meetings will cut down on daily interruptions from both sides.

✘ During the daily meetings, give your boss a brief status report on delegated tasks. Yes, it would be easier to let your boss assume you're getting things done, but there are times when he/she needs or wants to be in the know. A simple update prevents interruptions and makes your boss confident that you're on top of things, especially relating to important clients.

✗ Instead of leaning on your boss, take charge. Think about how you manage the office when your boss is gone. Do you handle things capably and accomplish a lot on your own? When your boss returns, however, do you suddenly ask loads of questions and use your boss as a crutch? If so, he/she might wonder why sometimes you're up to the task, and other times, you're not. If you're inconsistent and involve your boss in too many things, your initiative and competence will be questioned.

When you start to think like your boss -- which is the mark of a great employee -- you'll instinctively know how to make things easier. As Norman Vincent Peale said, "Change your thoughts and change the world." Whether dealing with your boss or the clients, challenge yourself to go above and beyond what's asked of you. That's taking the initiative!

In a nutshell, taking ownership means excelling at your job, while taking the initiative involves going above and beyond what's expected of you. If you really want to make your mark, adjust your thinking and grab the reins! Always be one step ahead, doing things without your boss's involvement (you're capable!) and prioritizing the things that need to get done. Be positive and proactive. As Henry Ford said, "If you think you can, you can. And if you think you can't, you're right."

OVERVIEW

✘ Put yourself in your employer's shoes. It's easier to take the initiative when you understand the daily challenges faced by your boss.

✘ Keep at it. Understand your boss's reluctance to hand over the reins, but keep plugging away. Your drive and ability will wear down the resistance.

✘ Remember the most important question, "What else can I do?" Pitch in!

✘ Speak up. If your boss is a micromanager, explain why you are perfectly capable of handling the job yourself.

8. Drawbacks of ROUTINE

"I wasn't losing my focus but I was getting tired of focusing. What I was focusing on was becoming too routine, too ritual, not something that was interesting, new and exciting."

Picabo Street

For those of you with years of experience at your current job, I offer some additional advice and a word of caution. Although you're a seasoned employee and what I've written may seem somewhat elementary, you need to watch out for the daily routines and attitudes that can derail a good business team.

Every day, I work with established teams struggling with poor communication, clogged workflow, lack of staff involvement and stalled growth. Once an employee gets past the three to five-year mark, things seem to change.

How? Often employees...

✗ become comfortable/complacent with their role; are unconcerned about growth and closed off to new ideas

✗ are resentful about their boss's lack of appreciation

- ✗ are adamant about making more money although they don't want to do more
- ✗ do their job, but lack initiative; get bogged down by work and don't try to expand their knowledge
- ✗ continue to get frustrated by constant change
- ✗ don't think outside the box; wait for directions instead of doing something on their own

Do any of these apply to you? If so, you probably need to change your thought process and attitude. Believe me, as an administrative assistant for 17 years, I had some of those feelings at various points in my career. I discovered, however, that they were counterproductive.

As I grew with the job, I learned to welcome new ideas, find different resources, expand my knowledge and be grateful for the opportunity to work in a small, successful business. Because of my take-charge approach, my job was never boring, I earned more money and truly made a difference, even if I didn't get much feedback from my boss.

If you're comfortable with your role and lack the need or desire to grow, it may be time to look for a new job. As a consultant, I often hear employers complain about their staff's complacency. They want more from their employees! Most business owners try to improve their own knowledge, sales capabilities or systems; they want their employees to keep moving as well. As the business evolves, employers want to delegate more to their staff.

If you're feeling resentful and unappreciated, you need to speak up. I'm not defending your boss, but so often employers are poor at giving praise or recognition. I remember one day asking my boss why he never told me I was doing a good job. Why didn't he acknowledge my efforts when I came in early or stayed late? He replied, "I could ask the same of you."

I had to think about that for a minute. He was right. I complained about things he did or didn't do when it affected my work, but if he did a great job at getting me referrals to call or stopped interrupting me so I could get my work done, I didn't say anything. From that point on, I learned we were both there to give 110%. By doing so we had mutual respect and appreciation for what we did. I also began to acknowledge the little things he did, and vice versa.

Your attitude is everything. I love this quote from Wayne Dyer. "Be miserable. Or motivate yourself. Whatever has to be done, it's always your choice." To earn the extras, you need to be willing to do more.

Money is always a touchy subject for both the employer and

employee. How often should you get a raise and why? What's it based on? Should you get a raise when the business isn't growing?

As an employee I expected a raise every year. On my one-year work anniversary, I asked for a raise and was shocked when my employer asked why I deserved one. My response: "I've been here for a year and I work hard." His response: "That's what I expect of you." Feeling defeated, I assumed I wasn't going to get a raise but I did. Even though I got a raise, I didn't feel it reflected my involvement or commitment. What if I wanted more? I took some time to think about this and eventually proposed an incentive plan based on my performance. We agreed that at the end of each year, we'd come up with two or three *new* goals I needed to accomplish to earn a raise. The goals involved continuing education, new technology, greater responsibility, etc. With this compensation plan, I knew what was expected of me, and if I achieved my goals, my income would grow in real value.

Can you do more to earn a raise? Remember in Chapter Five when I discussed SPFs? There's always more you can do by increasing the way you support, protect, filter or schedule your employer. If you're just doing your job and don't feel the need to go beyond what's expected of you, you probably won't be there long term.

In many offices, veteran employees can still get overwhelmed by constant change and unpredictability. Well, you may not want to hear this, but that's common. Most employers love change, challenge and new ventures. Many employees, however, like comfort and consistency. Allowing employers to be who they are and finding ways to adapt to their management styles will only improve teamwork.

If you're frustrated with your employer, just remember, that's not their intent. It's just how they operate. We can't change who we (or who they are) but we can learn to accept, acknowledge and grow side by side. You can have an amazing career by looking at things through your boss's eyes and taking the initiative to achieve greater success.

OVERVIEW

✗ Fight against complacency and rigid routines! If you're too set in your ways, you'll miss out on new and better approaches to work.

✗ If you want a raise, figure out a way to *earn* it.

✗ Choose your attitude. Your employer might be a saint or a handful, but either way, your outlook makes a difference on how much you bring to your job.

9. SCRIPTS for Taking the Initiative

"When we speak, we are afraid our words will not be heard or welcomed. But when we are silent, we are still afraid. So it is better to speak."

Audre Lorde

Many employers are as reluctant as you are to bring up certain issues in the workplace. They stumble around for words and are afraid of gaffes and misunderstandings. But regular communication is required if you plan to take the initiative at work. So think carefully and deliberately about what you want to say. As someone said, "The words you choose are just as important as the decision to speak."

Here are some scripts that can help you with various situations in the office.

You're not getting enough information from your boss to do your work.

"I need a little more information to complete the work on _____. Is now a good time to review that with me?"

Or

"We keep missing key points with the delegated work. How can I help you give me the information I need to get things done as quickly as possible?"

Your boss is not letting go.

"I've noticed you're doing things I can or should do for you. What are your concerns about me handling this task?"

Or

"Is there anything else I could be doing for you?"

Or

"I know it's not easy for you to let go of certain tasks. However, I feel it's counterproductive for you to be doing them. That's why I'm here. What can I do to assure you I can handle more?"

Your boss is micromanaging.

"I'm feeling good about my involvement in the business. However, I feel there are times when you second guess what I'm doing. Would you like me to prioritize things differently?"

Or

"I feel there are times when you trust me to do the work and believe in my abilities, yet there are other times when you question what I'm doing. What are you worried about?"

Your boss's last-minute delegation is creating some problems.

"I want to be sure things are prepared and accurate so you can review everything before your meetings, and you are totally present for the client."

Or

"How can I help you delegate in advance?"

Or

"Just an FYI, I don't do well with last minute delegations. My preference would be to prepare for your meetings a couple of days in advance to be sure you're totally prepared. How can I help you do that?"

Your boss often changes his/her mind on how something should be done.

"Over the past couple of months, we've been doing things one way, and now you want them done differently. Is this a permanent change, and if so why? I just want to understand to better support you."

You want a review/raise.

"It's been over a year since we've talked about my performance and compensation. Can we schedule a time to do so?"

Or

"To be sure we stay on the same page, I'd like to schedule a performance review every quarter. How does that sound to you?"

Your boss has overlooked something or made a mistake.

"I know you're really busy, but I want to make sure this is what you meant in this letter." (Or illustration, PowerPoint presentation, etc.)

Using these scripts is a form of taking the initiative. By bringing up problems or situations, you're taking action. Instead of waiting for a cue from your boss, you're moving forward to find solutions. Remember, you're the safety net for and reflection of your boss. Don't hesitate to bring something up even if you're afraid to. If you don't, it could lead to a bigger problem or embarrassment for someone.

Speak up and go for it! As Lee Trevino observed, "You can have brilliant ideas, but if you can't get them across, your ideas won't get you anywhere."

FINAL THOUGHTS

Take Initiative & Succeed! is a companion piece to *Let Go & Lead!*, my earlier book on how to become a better boss. When the two publications are read together, you get the full picture of effective teamwork. It's a balance: The employer lets go and delegates work consistently while the staff takes the initiative to free up the employer's time for income-producing activities.

Believe me, I'm not saying employees should do all the work or carry a heavier burden than their boss. I make it clear in *Let Go & Lead!* that employees deserve respect and a positive work experience. What I am saying is that you should work together with your boss to create the most successful team possible. Discover your purpose at work, and you'll be rewarded with job satisfaction, challenge and financial reward.

Maybe some parts of the book don't apply to you right now, but things change, and some of my ideas might come in handy in the future. You can refer to this book whenever you need to take the initiative at work. Your actions and attitude will determine your success!

Gina Pellegrini is the owner of Pellegrini Team Consulting, a Minneapolis-based firm specializing in team building and leadership development. For nearly 20 years, Gina has worked with business owners to streamline systems, increase productivity, strengthen accountability and improve communication. With Gina's help, employers become better leaders, and employees become more involved in the company vision, decision-making and growth.

Gina hosts two teleconferences series, **The Revenue Resource**, a program designed to sharpen the phone skills of marketing assistants, and **The Ultimate Team**, a group series on effective leadership and team performance. In addition to *Let Go & Lead!*, her products include *The Appointment Scheduler, The Wisdom of TeamWork, The Power of Two and The Personnel Package*. Gina has been featured in various trade magazines and has spoken at the Court of the Table, MDRT, NAIFA and the Conference for African American Financial Professionals.

Before starting her business, Gina was an administrative/marketing assistant for 17 years for a top financial producer in Chicago. She has drawn on that experience to design successful teamwork programs for clients throughout the United States and Canada.

The Ultimate Team

We'll help you build it!

The Ultimate Team is designed for teams that want more – more enthusiasm, clarity, communication and teamwork. In a series of group phones calls, Gina teaches your team how to get bigger and better results by streamlining workflow, eliminating interruptions and holding your team accountable.

Benefits for producers...
- overcome the fear of letting go
- develop greater trust in your employees
- learn to delegate more effectively
- eliminate voicemail and email
- toss out your In Box
- be more prepared and visionary

Benefits for staff...
- become more involved in the company vision
- learn to take the initiative
- work without interruptions
- use one to-do list
- improve team communication
- know who's doing what and why

To register for this series contact us at (952) 829-5300

The Revenue Resource
Are you sitting on a gold mine?

In The Revenue Resource, Gina explains how to dig deeper into your client base to uncover new opportunities and more revenue. The group calls with Gina sharpen your staff's phone skills and produce a better, more consistent appointment stream.

Benefits for producers...
- let go of all your calls
- work your client base proactively
- obtain more referrals
- follow an Ideal Week

Benefits for staff...
- leave effective messages
- increase return calls
- overcome objections
- gain confidence and professionalism

To register for this series contact us at (952) 829-5300